W9-BZP-520

HOW I LEARNED TO RIDE THE BICYCLE

*–Reflections of an influential
19th century woman–*

Frances E. Willard

Introduction by Edith Mayo
Smithsonian Institution

Edited by Carol O'Hare

FAIR OAKS PUBLISHING
Sunnyvale, California

Design by Susan Cronin-Paris

Published by Fair Oaks Publishing Company
941 Populus Place
Sunnyvale, CA 94086
(408) 732-1078

Willard, Frances Elizabeth, 1839-1898.
  How I learned to ride the bicycle : reflections of an influential
19th century woman / by Frances E. Willard ; introduction by
Edith Mayo ; edited by Carol O'Hare.
        p.   cm.
  Rev. ed. of: A wheel within a wheel. 1895.
  Includes bibliographical references.
  ISBN 0-933271-04-2 (alk. paper) : $14.95
  ISBN 0-933271-05-0 (alk. paper) :   8.95 (pbk.)
  1. Cycling for women. 2. Willard, Frances Elizabeth, 1839-
1898. I. O'Hare, Carol. II. Willard, Frances Elizabeth, 1839-
1898. Wheel within a wheel. III. Title.
GV1057.W73   1991
796.6'082—dc20   90-19367
                                                              CIP

The paper used in this publication meets the minimum requirements of American
National Standard for Information Sciences—Permanence of Paper for Printed Library
Materials, ANSI Z39.48-1984.
                                                    ∞

How I Learned
to ride the Bicycle

Frances E Willard

Gratefully Dedicated

to

Lady Henry Somerset,

who gave me "Gladys,"

that harbinger of health and happiness.

Table of Contents

Introduction: "Do Everything"
The Life and Work of Frances Willard
by Edith Mayo   1

How I Learned to Ride the Bicycle

Preliminary   15

The Process   25

My Teachers   41

An Ethereal Episode   67

In Conclusion   73

Notes   79

Women and Cycling: The Early Years
by Lisa Larrabee   81

Bibliography   99

About the Authors   103

"Do Everything"
The Life and Work of Frances Willard
(1839-1898)

by Edith Mayo

Frances Willard is little known to the public today, but in her own time, she was one of the most famous and charismatic figures in national life. Born in western New York to strict Methodist parents, she grew up on the prairie near Janesville, Wisconsin, where her father had moved the family to live and work in the outdoors, in an attempt to improve his health. Frances spent her childhood on the frontier as a "tomboy." She was remarkably free of the usual feminine behavioral constraints, and spared the endless cooking, cleaning, and needlework chores of girls of her day. She wore her hair short, insisted on being called "Frank," and enjoyed a "romping" girlhood. "Living in the country, far from the artificial restraints and conventions by which most girls are hedged . . . I 'ran wild' until my sixteenth birthday," she recalled.

At sixteen, life changed. From then on she wore the "hampering long skirts," corset, and high heels required of young women her age. Little schooling was available to Frances in her early years, yet her family encouraged her to read and provided an atmosphere of intellectual curiosity. In 1857 she began attending Milwaukee Female College, but her father insisted that she transfer to North Western Female College in Evanston, Illinois, a school affiliated with the Methodist Church. By this time, her family had moved to Evanston, which remained her home for the rest of her life.

After graduation from college, Frances Willard found herself restless and unsettled. She at first followed the traditional path of most women toward marriage and had a short, but traumatic, engagement to Charles Henry Fowler, pastor of a Chicago Methodist church and a friend and theological school classmate of her brother. At one point Fowler told her that he intended to go to China as a missionary, seeking to know whether she would accompany him. She was deeply troubled, prayed about her decision and, after determining to go with him, was told that he had been merely "testing her love." Angered by his cruel deception which had caused her so much pain, she broke the engagement.

Willard had also felt very keenly her father's domination of family life and was determined to be independent. She entered teaching, one of the few professions open to women at that time, and held a series of positions at Methodist schools in the Midwest. In 1870 she became president of the Evanston College for Ladies, a school closely affiliated with Northwestern University. Three years later the college was wholly taken over by Northwestern, whose new president was Charles Fowler, Willard's former fiance. Willard was retained as Dean of Women and Professor of English at Northwestern. Fowler, however, proved to be a domineering president, and bitter disputes ensued between the two about the extent of Willard's jurisdiction over the women students at the University. After a series of petty challenges to her authority, Willard resigned in 1874. At thirty-five, she was without a profession, without savings, and deeply unhappy.

It was at this time that Frances Willard became involved with the causes that would be her life's work. She had already been attracted to the woman's movement, having been elected vice president of the Association for the Advancement of Women, an organization sponsored by the pioneer New York woman's club, Sororis.

The Temperance Movement

In the mid-1870's popular sentiment for temperance reform (which strove for voluntary renunciation of liquor and laws to restrict or abolish its sale and manufacture) was sweeping the Midwestern states. A newly formed Chicago temperance group asked Willard to be their leader and delegate to the Cleveland, Ohio, convention that founded the Woman's Christian Temperance Union (WCTU) in 1874. She was elected corresponding secretary for the new organization and soon came to know all the leaders of state and local WCTU chapters.

Her ambition, strong organizational abilities, and reform tendencies brought her into conflict with Annie Wittenmyer, first president of the national WCTU. Because of these strained relations, in 1877 Willard resigned her WCTU post to take a position in support of the ministry of evangelist Dwight L. Moody in Boston. Finding his orthodoxy too constricting, Willard returned to Evanston, bringing with her Anna Gordon, who became her lifelong secretary and beloved companion. She resumed her involvement with the WCTU and was elected president of the Illinois chapter. Under her leadership, a state-wide temperance petition campaign gained the signatures of more than one hundred thousand women and became a model for WCTU actions throughout the states. Its success brought

Willard back into the spotlight, and in 1879 she was elected president of the national WCTU, a position she held for the remaining twenty years of her life.

The temperance movement was a response to the growing problem of alcoholism, a major social concern in the late nineteenth century. Most women of that time were dependent on a husband's wages for economic support. They had few legal rights and no welfare system available to them. For them, an alcoholic husband was a family disaster. Alcoholism not only devastated the family's economic support, it often brought with it the child and spouse abuse familiar in today's headlines but then only whispered about. Alcoholism struck at the heart of home and family, which were, as both religious and popular belief held, the Divinely-ordained special province of women. Women, therefore, viewed alcoholism as a very direct threat to their personal and familial safety, as well as to their realm of power.

This threat galvanized women into action. After a series of moving temperance lectures by the Reverend Dio Lewis in 1873, women in Hillsboro, Ohio, left their homes and took to the streets in direct protest against saloons. Praying (a pioneering form of picketing) and singing hymns, women became a familiar sight at liquor establishments throughout the Midwest. Women "going about Our Father's business" intimidated owners and patrons alike, and successfully closed many saloons. In Cincinnati, a major liquor distribution center, liquor dealers fought back, obtaining court injunctions against women singing hymns and praying in saloons. Many women refused to disperse and were arrested. Like the suffragists and civil rights workers after them, the women considered their jailing a badge of honor. Clearly, this movement had exposed women's dormant rage and engendered a life-long commitment to reform.

Tapping both these sources of women's energy, the Woman's Christian Temperance Union organized thousands in its crusade against the sale and consumption of alcohol, which it linked with poverty, social corruption, and the degradation of family life. As guardians of the home, women believed they had a special mission to bring moral family values into public life.

Politics and Reform

Frances Willard, during her two decades of leadership of the WCTU, used her superb political skills to make it the largest women's organization of the nineteenth century and the vanguard of progressive reform. Her political genius combined organizational talent, rhetorical prowess, and personal charisma. She possessed the ability to lead basically conservative, anti-political church women gradually into public action, using the language of women's traditional roles as guardians and defenders of their homes and families. The WCTU provided Willard and her followers a large, grass-roots organization, structured by women and free of the influence and domination of men, as a base of operation. Its church-related nature lent respectability and unquestioned social sanction to actions that would have been criticized as blatantly political had they been undertaken in another context. Working through Protestant church networks, Willard and the WCTU called to action large numbers of church women, expanded women's role in society, and demanded that they share in the political process.

But Willard worked for other reforms as well. Realizing that alcoholism resulted as much from social ills as from moral or personal lapses, and that ending the liquor traffic required more than "moral suasion," Willard gradually led the WCTU to a demand for the "Home Protection Ballot" (her euphemistic and unthreatening term for woman suffrage) in an attempt to obtain legislation for social reform.

Couched in Christian rhetoric, Willard's gospel politics inspired temperance workers to "Do Everything" in their crusade for social justice. In addition to working for laws against liquor, Willard urged followers to support prison reform, public kindergartens, child care for working mothers, and facilities for dependent and neglected children. She encouraged them to support industrial job training for young women and organized labor in their fight for the eight-hour working day. She advocated "social purity" (work against prostitution and venereal disease) and promoted world peace and international arbitration. In these efforts, Willard and the WCTU presaged and laid the ground work for some of the twentieth century's most important reform agendas, and for women's central and crucial involvement in those reforms.

Using women's role in the home and family as a rationale, Willard and the WCTU effectively organized women for direct political action. The "Do Everything" policy allowed the WCTU highly centralized national control, yet encouraged autonomy and innovation at the local level. While maintaining a tight hierarchical structure, whose national leadership set policy at yearly conventions, the WCTU then permitted local chapters to choose among a broad platform of reform causes. In one case, aggressive petitioning and lobbying efforts by the WCTU secured the passage of laws in 20 states raising the "age of legal consent" (to sexual relations for women) to sixteen. In some states the legal age had formerly been as low as seven years of age! In similar campaigns the WCTU was responsible for laws mandating instruction in "scientific temperance" and in physiology and personal hygiene (so that women would understand the working of their own bodies) in the schools in every state by 1901.

Willard believed in women's right to vote and built strong political alliances with the woman suffrage movement. She was also actively involved with the Prohibition Party, which advocated a constitutional amendment banning the manufacture and sale of liquor.

Willard's leadership style was both practical and innovative, and included availing herself and the WCTU of the latest advances in technology and a wide range of popular culture materials to promote her cause. For example, Willard used a dictaphone to ease the heavy correspondence burden and paperwork required of her as national president. As part of its media campaign, the WCTU circulated temperance songsters (temperance sentiments set to popular Protestant church hymns), produced posters with madonna-like mother and child images and the plea "Help Me to Keep Him Pure / Please Vote Against the Sale of Liquors," and used the then-new celluloid buttons familiar from political election campaigns with pictures of children and the slogan "Vote No for My Sake." These items focused on women's concern for their homes and children and projected them into the political arena without violating the notion of women's "proper" roles.

Taking reform to the international level, Willard was instrumental in creating a World Woman's Temperance Union, where she met Lady Henry Somerset, head of the British Women's Temperance Association. In 1892 Frances, shaken by the death of her mother and exhausted from years of traveling, organizing and lecturing, accepted an invitation to rest at her new friend's home, Eastnor Castle, in England. Here she was freed from bureaucratic responsibilities and the restraints of her more conservative American colleagues. Her innate intellectual curiosity was renewed, and she found a congenial circle of reformers among Lady Somerset's friends. Her gradual shift toward more radical politics, as evidenced in her growing political alliances and advocacy of radical reform at home, was confirmed when she joined the Fabian Socialists in England. She declared herself a Christian Socialist and admitted that "under the mould of conservative action I have been most radical in thought."

A Wider World

It was during this time that Lady Somerset presented Willard with a bicycle (nicknamed "Gladys"). In 1893 Frances Willard was fifty-three years old and not in good health, but she was determined to learn to ride. She was still willing to dare and take chances and urged others to do so also.

It was important to her that women take to the bicycle, and she believed her enthusiastic example would help lead women into new paths of life—ever expanding their horizons outward into the wider world. She was convinced that the thrill and exhilaration of mastering control of the bicycle would be matched by the sense of accomplishment a woman could experience in mastering control of her own personal destiny—quite a radical sentiment for that time.

In 1894 after returning to the United States, Willard's health began to fail, as a result of chronic pernicious anemia. In addition to her illness, she was faced with challenges to her growing radicalism and to her leadership of the WCTU. Yet, she retained the love of the rank and file members who continued to re-elect her president. At the time of her death in 1898, she was hailed as America's "heroine," "Queen of Temperance," and the "foremost woman in public life."

As president of the Woman's Christian Temperance Union, Frances Willard built the largest national organization of women of the nineteenth century. The WCTU, which Willard termed "a sisterhood of the women's party," served as a pioneering national political voice for women. Understanding the importance of the temperance movement to women, Willard declared, "This work has tended more toward the liberation of women than . . . toward the extinction of the saloon."

A Wheel Within a Wheel

Willard's experience in learning to ride the bicycle is described in this delightful book, originally titled, *A Wheel Within a Wheel*. Published in 1895, it quickly became a best seller and no doubt encouraged other women to take up the bicycle. Willard's fascination with the new and innovative, her love of a challenge, and her desire to feel a sense of mastery were all encompassed in learning to ride.

Although her writing style betrays more than a little of the old schoolteacher, *How I Learned to Ride the Bicycle* epitomizes her approach to her constituency, honed through the years, of teaching through parables. She employs the same technique she used with women to make political activity palatable, cleverly bringing along her readers by acknowledging the weight of public opinion against a new activity for women and then, one by one, demolishing the objections with a common sense approach.

In her writing, the bicycle and its techniques of mastery become an extended metaphor for life itself. The principles by which one masters riding the bicycle are those by which one masters life, marriage, and family. And these principles become a philosophy for the "right" living of one's life. The mastery is within oneself, and not simply in the techniques of mounting, learning to balance, and dismounting the machine.

Continuing her parable on life, Willard extends the qualities and characteristics necessary to master the bicycle to those needed to advance reforms. She compares the frustrations of learning to ride on days of no gain to times when reforms lag behind. Other times, both bicycle mastery and reforms move ahead. Both come from continued perseverance and developing skills.

As with all her endeavors, Frances Willard turned learning to ride the bicycle into a liberating experience for women.

I called my bicycle Gladys, having in view the
exhilarating motion of the machine, and the gladdening effect of its acquaintance and use on my health.

How I Learned to Ride the Bicycle

Preliminary

ROM my earliest recollections, and up
to the ripe age of fifty-three, I had been an
active and diligent worker in the world. This
sounds absurd; but having almost no toys except
such as I could manufacture, my first plays were
but the outdoor work of active men and women
on a small scale. Born with an inveterate
opposition to staying in the house, I very early
learned to use a carpenter's kit and a gardener's
tools, and followed in my mimic way the
occupations of the poulterer and the farmer,

working my little field with a wooden plow of my own making, and felling saplings with an ax rigged up from the old iron of the wagon-shop. Living in the country, far from the artificial restraints and conventions by which most girls are hedged from the activities that would develop a good physique, and endowed with the companionship of a mother who let me have my own sweet will, I "ran wild" until my sixteenth birthday, when the hampering long skirts were brought, with their accompanying corset and high heels; my hair was clubbed up with pins, and I remember writing in my journal, in the first heartbreak of a young human colt taken from its pleasant pasture, "Altogether, I recognize that my occupation is gone."

From that time on I always realized and was obedient to the limitations thus imposed, though in my heart of hearts I felt their unwisdom even more than their injustice. My work then changed from my beloved and breezy outdoor world to the indoor realm of study, teaching, writing, speaking, and went on almost without a break or pain until my fifty-third year, when the loss of my mother accentuated the strain of this long period in which mental and physical life were out of balance, and I fell into a mild form of what is called nerve-wear by the patient and nervous prostration by the lookers-on. Thus ruthlessly thrown out of the usual lines of reaction with my environment, and sighing for new worlds to conquer, I determined that I would learn the bicycle.

An English naval officer had said to me, after learning it himself, "You women have no idea of the new realm of happiness which the bicycle has opened to us men." Already I knew well enough that tens of thousands who could never afford to own, feed, and stable a horse, had by this bright invention enjoyed the swiftness of motion which is perhaps the most fascinating feature of material life, the charm of a wide outlook upon the natural world, and that sense of mastery which is probably the greatest attraction in horseback-riding. But the bicycle is the steed that never tires, and is "mettlesome" in the fullest sense of the word. It is full of tricks and capers, and to hold his head steady

and make him prance to suit you is no small
accomplishment. I had often mentioned in my
temperance writings that the bicycle was
perhaps our strongest ally in winning young men
away from public-houses, because it afforded
them a pleasure far more enduring, and an
exhilaration as much more delightful as the
natural is than the unnatural. From my observation of my own brother and hundreds of young
men who have been my pupils, I have always
held that a boy's heart is not set in him to do
evil any more than a girl's, and that the reason
our young men fall into evil ways is largely
because we have not had the wit and wisdom to
provide them with amusements suited to their
joyous youth, by means of which they could
invest their superabundant animal spirits in
ways that should harm no one and help themselves to the best development and the cleanli-
est ways of living. So as a temperance reformer I
always felt a strong attraction toward the
bicycle, because it is the vehicle of so much
harmless pleasure, and because the skill required
in handling it obliges those who mount to keep

clear heads and steady hands. Nor could I see a
reason in the world why a woman should not
ride the silent steed so swift and blithesome. I
knew perfectly well that when, some ten or
fifteen years ago, Miss Bertha von Hillern, a
young German artist in America, took it into
her head to give exhibitions of her skill in riding
the bicycle, she was thought by some to be a sort
of semi-monster; and liberal as our people are in
their views of what a woman may undertake, I
should certainly have felt compromised, at that
remote and benighted period, by going to see
her ride, not because there was any harm in it,
but solely because of what we call in homely
phrase "the speech of people." But behold! it
was long ago conceded that women might ride
the tricycle—indeed, one had been presented to
me by my friend Colonel Pope, of Boston, a
famous manufacturer of these swift roadsters, as
far back as 1886; and I had swung around the
garden paths upon its saddle a few minutes every
evening when work was over at my Rest Cottage home.[1] I had even hoped to give an
impetus among conservative women to this new

line of physical development and outdoor happiness; but that is quite another story and will come in later. Suffice it for the present that it did me good, as it doth the upright in heart, to notice recently that the Princesses Louise and Beatrice both ride the tricycle at Balmoral; for I know that with the great mass of feminine humanity this precedent will have exceeding weight—and where the tricycle prophesies, the bicycle shall ere long preach the gospel of the outdoors.

For we are all unconsciously the slaves of public opinion. When the hansom carriage first came on London streets no woman having regard to her social state and standing would have dreamed of entering one of these pavement gondolas unless accompanied by a gentleman as her escort. But in course of time a few women, of stronger individuality than the average, ventured to go unattended; later on, use wore off the glamour of the traditions which said that women must not go alone, and now none but an imbecile would hold herself to any such observance.

A trip around the world by a young woman would have been regarded a quarter of a century ago as equivalent to social outlawry; but now young women of the highest character and talent are employed by leading journals to whip around the world "on time," and one has done so in seventy-three days, another in seventy-four, while the young women recently sent out by an Edinburgh newspaper will no doubt considerably contract these figures.

As I have mentioned, Fraulein von Hillern is the first woman, so far as I know, who ever rode a bicycle, and for this she was considered to be an outcast in all classes and a traitor to the feminine guild; but now, in France, for a woman to ride a bicycle is not only "good form," but the current craze among the aristocracy.

There has been but little authentic talking done by four-footed animals; but that is no reason why the two-wheeled should not speak its mind, and the first utterance I have to chronicle in the softly flowing vocables of my bicycle is to the following purport. I heard it as we trundled off down the Priory incline at the suburban home of Lady Henry Somerset[2] in Reigate, England, where I was staying. It said: "Behold, I do not fail you; I am not a skittish beastie, but a sober, well-conducted roadster. I did not ask you to mount or drive, but since you have done so you must now learn the laws of balance and exploitation. I did not invent these laws, but I have been built to conform to them, and you must suit yourself to the unchanging regulations of gravity, general and specific, as illustrated in me. Strange as the paradox may seem, you will do this best by not trying to do it at all. You must make up what you are pleased to call your mind—make it up speedily, or you will be cast in yonder mud puddle, and no blame to me and no thanks to yourself. Two things must occupy your thinking powers to the exclusion of every other thing: first, the goal; and, second, the momentum requisite to reach it. Do not look down like an imbecile upon the steering wheel in front of you—that would be about as wise as for a nauseated voyager to keep his optical instruments fixed upon the rolling waves. It is the curse of life that nearly every one looks down. But the microscope will never set you free; you must glue your eyes to the telescope forever and a day. Look up and off and on and out; get forehead and foot into line, the latter acting as a rhythmic spur in the flanks of your equilibriated equine; so shall you win, and that right speedily.

"It was divinely said that the kingdom of God is within you. Some make a mysticism of this declaration, but it is hard common sense; for the lesson you will learn from me is this: every kingdom over which we reign must be first formed within us on what I as a bicycle look upon as the common parade ground of individual thought."

Three young Englishmen, all strong-armed and accomplished bicyclers, held the machine in place while I climbed timidly into the saddle.

The Process

 ourtiers wittily say that horseback riding is the only thing in which a prince is apt to excel, for the reason that the horse never flatters and would as soon throw him as if he were a groom. Therefore it is only by actually mastering the art of riding that a prince can hold his place with the noblest of the four-footed animals.

Happily there is now another locomotive contrivance which is no flatterer, and which peasant and prince must master, if they do this at all, by the democratic route of honest hard work. We all know the old saying, "Fire is a good servant, but a bad master." This is equally true of the bicycle: if you give it an inch—nay, a hair—it will take a yard—nay, an evolution—and you a contusion, or, like enough, a perforated kneecap.

Not a single friend encouraged me to learn the bicycle except an active-minded young schoolteacher, Miss Luther, in my hometown of Evanston, who came several times with her wheel and gave me lessons. I also took a few lessons in a stuffy, semi-subterranean gallery in Chicago. But at fifty-three I was at more disadvantage than most people, for not only had I the impedimenta that result from the unnatural style of dress, but I also suffered from the sedentary habits of a lifetime. And then that small world (which is our real one) of those who loved me best, and who considered themselves largely responsible for my everyday methods of life, did not encourage me, but in their affectionate solicitude—and with abundant reason—thought I should "break my bones" and "spoil my future." It must be said, however, to their everlasting praise, that they posed no objection when they saw that my will was firmly set to do this thing; on the contrary, they put me in the way of carrying out my purpose, and lent to my laborious lessons the light of their countenances reconciled. Actions speak so much louder than words that I here set before you what may be called a feminine bicycler's inauguration—at least it was mine.

While staying in England, I set out to learn the safety-bicycle with its pneumatic tires and all the rest, the gearing carefully wired in so that we shall not be entangled. "Woe is me!" was my first exclamation, naturally enough interpreted by my outriders "Whoa is me," and they "whoaed"—indeed, we did little else but "check up."

The order of evolution was something like this: first, three young Englishmen, all strong-armed and accomplished bicyclers, held the machine in place while I climbed timidly into the saddle. In the second stage of my learning, two well-disposed young women put in all the power they had, until they grew red in the face, off-setting each other's pressure on the cross-bar and thus maintaining the equipoise to which I was unequal. Thirdly, one walked beside me, steadying the ark as best she could by holding the center of the deadly cross-bar, to let go whose handles meant chaos and collapse. Eventually I was able to hold my own if I had the moral support of my kind trainers, and it passed into a proverb among them, the short emphatic word of command I gave them at every few turns of the wheel: "Let go, but stand by." Still later everything was learned—how to sit, how to pedal, how to turn, how to dismount; but alas! how to vault into the saddle I found not; that was the coveted power that lingered long and would not yield itself.

That which caused the many failures I had in learning the bicycle had caused me failures in life; namely, a certain fearful looking for of judgment; a too vivid realization of the uncertainty of everything about me; an underlying doubt—at once, however (and this is all that saved me), matched and overcome by the determination not to give in to it.

The best gains that we make come to us after an interval of rest which follows strenuous endeavor. Having, as I hoped, mastered the rudiments of bicycling, I went away to Germany and for a fortnight did not even see the winsome wheel. Returning, I had the machine brought round, and mounted with no little trepidation, being assisted by one of my faithful guides; but behold! I found that in advancing, turning, and descending I was much more at home than when I had last exercised that new intelligence in the muscles which had been the result of repetitions resolutely attempted and practiced long.

Another thing I found is that we carry in the mind a picture of the road; and if it is bumpy by reason of pebbles, even if we steer clear of them, we can by no means skim along as happily as when its smoothness facilitates the pleasing impression on the retina; indeed, the whole science and practice of the bicycle is "in your eye" and in your will; the rest is mere manipulation.

As I have said, in many curious particulars the bicycle is like the world. When it had thrown me painfully once (which was the extent of my downfalls during the entire process of learning, and did not prevent me from resuming my place on the back of the treacherous creature a few minutes afterward), and more especially when it threw one of my dearest friends, hurting her knee so that it was painful for a month, then for a time Gladys (the name I had given my bicycle) had gladsome ways for me no longer, but seemed the embodiment of misfortune and dread. Even so the world has often seemed in hours of darkness and despondency; its iron mechanism, its pitiless grind, its swift, silent, on-rolling gait have oppressed to pathos, if not to melancholy. Fortunately, good health and plenty of oxygenated air have promptly restored the equilibrium.

Gradually, item by item, I learned the location of every screw and spring, spoke and tire, and every beam and bearing that went to make up Gladys. This was not the lesson of a day, but of many days and weeks, and it had to be learned before we could get on well together. To my mind the infelicities of which we see so much in life grow out of lack of time and patience to study and adjust our natures to those of others, though we have agreed in the sight of

God and man to stand by one another to the last. Many will not take the pains, they have not enough specific gravity, to balance themselves in their new environment. Indeed, I found a whole philosophy of life in the wooing and the winning of my bicycle.

Just as a strong and skillful swimmer takes the waves, so the bicycler must learn to take such waves of mental impression as the passing of a gigantic haywagon, the sudden obtrusion of black cattle with wide-branching horns, the rattling pace of high-stepping steeds, or even the swift transit of a railway train. At first she will be upset by the apparition of the smallest poodle, and not until she has attained a wide experience will she hold herself steady in presence of a coach with four horses. But all this is a part of that equilibration of thought and action by which we conquer the universe in conquering ourselves.

I finally concluded that all failure was from a wobbling will rather than a wobbling wheel. I felt that indeed the will is the wheel of the mind— its perpetual motion having been learned when

the morning stars sang together. When the
wheel of the mind went well, then the rubber
wheel hummed merrily; but specters of the mind
there are as well as of the wheel. In the aggregate
of perception there are so many ghastly and
fantastical images that they must obtrude
themselves at certain intervals. Probably every
accident of which I had heard or read in my
half-century tinged the uncertainty that I felt
when we began to round the terminus bend of
the broad Priory walk. And who shall say by
what original energy the mind forced itself at
once from the contemplation of disaster and
thrust into the very movement of the foot on
the pedal a concept of vigor, safety, and success?
I began to feel that myself plus the bicycle
equaled myself plus the world, upon whose spinning wheel we must all learn to ride, or fall into
the sluiceways of oblivion and despair. That
which made me succeed with the bicycle was
precisely what had gained me a measure of
success in life—it was the hardihood of Spirit
that led me to begin, the persistence of will that
held me to my task, and the patience that was

willing to begin again when the last stroke had failed. And so I found high moral uses in the bicycle and can commend it as a teacher without pulpit or creed. He who succeeds, or, to be more exact in handing over my experience, she who succeeds in gaining the mastery of such an animal as Gladys, will gain the mastery of life, and by exactly the same methods and characteristics.

One of the first things I learned was that unless a forward impetus were given within well-defined intervals, away we went into the gutter, rider and steed. And I said to myself: "It is the same with all reforms: sometimes they seem to lag, then they barely balance, then they begin to oscillate as if they would lose the track and tumble to one side; but all they need is a new impetus at the right moment on the right angle, and away they go again as merrily as if they had never threatened to stop at all."

On the Castle terrace we went through a long, narrow curve in a turret to seek a broader esplanade. As we approached it I felt wrought up in my mind, a little uncertain in my motions; and for that reason, on a small scale, my quick imagination put before me pictures of damaging bruises against the pitiless walls. But with a little unobtrusive guiding by one who knew better than I how to do it we soon came out of the dim passage on to the broad, bright terrace we sought, and in an instant my fears were as much left behind as if I had not had them. So it will be, I think, I hope—nay, I believe—when, children that we are, we tremble on the brink and fear to launch away; but we shall find that death is only a bend in the river of life that sets the current heavenward.

One afternoon, on the terrace at Eastnor Castle—the most delightful bicycle gallery I have found anywhere—I fell to talking with a young companion about New Year resolutions. It was just before Christmas, but the sky was of that moist blue that England only knows, and the earth almost steamy in the mild sunshine, while the soft outline of the famous Malvern Hills was restful as the little lake just at our feet, where swans were sailing or anchoring according to their fancy.

One of us said: "I have already chosen my motto for 1894, and it is this: 'I have heard something nice about you.' It comes from a teacher who said it so often to her pupils, when meeting them in corridor or recitation room, that it passed into a proverb in the school. Now I have determined that my mental attitude toward everybody shall be the same that these words indicate. The meaning is identical with that of the inscription on the fireplace in my den at home—'Let something good be said.' I remember mentioning to a literary friend that this was what I had chosen, and so far was he from perceiving my intention that he sarcastically remarked, 'Are you then afraid that people will say dull things unless you set this rule before them?' But my thought then was as it is now, that we should apply in our discussions of people and things the rule laid down by Coleridge, namely, 'Look for the good in everything that you behold and every person, but do not decline to see the defects if they are there, and to refer to them.'"

"That is an excellent motto," brightly replied the other, "but if we followed it life would not be nearly so amusing as it is now. I have several friends whose rule is never to say any harm of anybody, and to my mind this cripples their development, for the tendency of such a method is to dull one's powers of discrimination."

"But," said the first speaker, "would not a medium course be better?—such a one, for instance, as my motto suggests. This would not involve keeping silence about the faults of persons and things, but would develop that cheerful atmosphere which helps to smooth the rough edges of life, and at the same time does not destroy the critical faculty, because you are to tell the truth and the whole truth concerning those around you, whereas the common custom is to speak much of defects and little or not at all of merits."

"Yes," was the reply, "but it is not half so entertaining to speak of virtues as of faults, especially in this country; if you don't criticize you can hardly talk at all, because the English dwell a great deal on what we in America call 'the selvage side' of things. I have noticed this as a national peculiarity after ten years of observation."

"What do you think explains it?"

"Well, I should say it was the climate; its uncertainty, its constant changes, the heaviness of the atmosphere, the amount of fog, the real stress and strain to live that results from trying physical conditions added to the razor-sharp edge of business and social competition and the close contact that comes of packing forty millions of people of pronounced individuality on an island no bigger than the State of Georgia. To my mind the wonder is that they behave so well!"

Once, when I grew somewhat discouraged and said that I had made no progress for a day or two, my teacher told me that it was just so when she learned: there were growing days and stationary days, and she had always noticed that just after one of these last dull, depressing, and dubious intervals she seemed to get an uplift and went ahead better than ever. It was like a spurt in rowing. This seems to be the law of progress in everything we do; it moves along a spiral rather than a perpendicular; we seem to be actu-

ally going out of the way, and yet it turns out
that we were really moving upward all the time.

One day, when my most expert trainer
twisted the truth a little that she might encourage me, I was reminded of an anecdote.

In this practical age an illustration of the
workings of truthfulness will often help a child
more than any amount of exhortation concerning the theory thereof. For instance, a father in
that level-headed part of the United States
known as "out West" found that his little boy
was falling into the habit of telling what was not
true; so he said to him at the lunch-table,
"Johnnie, I will come around with a horse and
carriage at four o'clock to take you and mama
for a drive this afternoon." The boy was in high
spirits, and watched for his father at the gate;
but the hours passed by until six o'clock, when
that worthy appeared walking up the street in
the most unconcerned manner; and when
Johnnie, full of indignation and astonishment,
asked him why he did not come as he had
promised, the father said, "Oh, my boy, I just
took it into my head that I would tell you a lie

about the matter, just as you have begun telling lies to me." The boy began to cry with mingled disappointment and shame to think his father would do a thing like that; whereupon the father took the little fellow on his knee and said: "This has all been done to show you what mischief comes from telling what is not true. It spoils everybody's good time. If you cannot believe what I say and I cannot believe what you say, and nobody can believe what any-body says, then the world cannot go on at all; it would have to stop as the old eight-day clock did the other day, making us all late to dinner. It is only because, as a rule, we can believe in one another's word that we are able to have homes, do business, and enjoy life. Whoever goes straight on telling the truth helps more by that than he could in any other one way to build up the world into a beautiful and happy place; and every time anybody tells what is not true he helps to weaken everybody's confidence in everybody else, and to spoil the good time, not of himself alone, but of all those about him."

It will be a delight to girls to learn that the fact of their sex is, in itself, not a bar to riding a wheel.

My Teachers

 studied my various kind teachers with much care. One was so helpful that but for my protest she would fairly have carried me in her arms, and the bicycle to boot, the whole distance. This was because she had not a scintilla of knowledge concerning the machine, and she did not wish me to come to grief through any lack on her part.

Another was too timorous; the very twitter of her face, swiftly communicated to her arm

and imparted to the quaking cross-bar, con-
vulsed me with an inward fear; therefore, for her
sake and mine, I speedily counted her out from
the faculty in my bicycle college. Another (and
she, like most of my teachers, was a Londoner)
was herself so capable, not to say adventurous,
and withal so solicitous for my best good, that
she elicited my admiration by her ingenious
mixture of cheering me on and holding me
back; the latter, however, predominated, for she
never relinquished her strong grasp on the cross-
bar. She was a fine, brave character, somewhat
inclined to a pessimistic view of life because of
severe experience at home, which, coming to
her at a pitifully early period, when brain and
fancy were most impressionable, wrought an
injustice to a nature large and generous—one
which under happier skies would have blos-
somed out into a perfect flower of womanhood.
My off hand thinkings aloud, to which I have
always been greatly given, especially when in
genial company, she seemed to "catch on the
fly," as a reporter impales an idea on his pencil-
point. We had no end of what we thought to be

good talk of things in heaven and earth and the waters under the earth; of the mystery that lies so closely round this cradle of a world, and all the varied and ingenious ways of which the bicycle, so slow to give up its secret to a care-worn and inelastic pupil half a century old, was just then our whimsical and favorite symbol.

We rejoiced together greatly in perceiving the impetus that this uncompromising but fascinating and illimitably capable machine would give to that blessed "woman question" to which we were both devoted; for we had earned our own bread many a year, and she, although more than twenty years my junior, had accumulated an amount of experience well-nigh as great because she had lived in the world's heart, or the world's carbuncle (as one may choose to regard what has been called in literary phrase the capital of humanity). We saw that the physical development of humanity's mother-half would be wonderfully advanced by that universal introduction of the bicycle sure to come about within the next few years. It is for the interest of great commercial monopolies that this should be so, since if women patronize the wheel the number of buyers will be twice as large. If women ride they must, when riding, dress more rationally than they have been wont to do. If they do this many prejudices as to what they may be allowed to wear will melt away. Reason will gain upon precedent, and ere long the comfortable, sensible, and artistic wardrobe of the rider will make the conventional style of woman's dress absurd to the eye and unendurable to the understanding. A reform often advances most rapidly by indirection. An ounce of practice is worth a ton of theory; and the graceful and becoming costume of woman on the bicycle will convince the world that has brushed aside the theories, no matter how well constructed, and the arguments, no matter how logical, of dress-reformers.

A woman with bands hanging on her hips, and dress snug about the waist and chokingly tight at the throat, with heavily trimmed skirts dragging down the back and numerous folds heating the lower part of the spine, and with tight shoes, ought to be in agony. She ought to be as miserable as a stalwart man would be in the same plight. And the fact that she can coolly and complacently assert that her clothing is perfectly easy, and that she does not want anything more comfortable or convenient, is the most conclusive proof that she is altogether abnormal bodily, and not a little so in mind.

We saw with satisfaction the great advantage in good fellowship and mutual understanding between men and women who take the road together, sharing its hardships and rejoicing in the poetry of motion through landscapes breathing nature's inexhaustible charm and skyscapes lifting the heart from what is to what shall be hereafter. We discoursed on the advantage to masculine character of comradeship with women who were as skilled and ingenious in the manipulation of the swift steed as they themselves. We contended that whatever diminishes the sense of superiority in men makes them more manly, brotherly, and pleasant to have about; we felt sure that the bluff, the swagger, the bravado of young men would not outlive the mastery of the outdoor arts in which his sister is now successfully engaged. The old fables, myths, and follies associated with the idea of woman's incompetence to handle bat and oar, bridle and rein, and at last the cross-bar of the bicycle, are passing into contempt in presence of her nimbleness, agility, and skill; indeed, we felt that if she continued to improve after the fashion of the last decade her physical achievements will be such that it will become the pride of many a ruddy youth to be known as "that girl's brother." As we discoursed of life, death, and the judgment to come, of "man's inhumanity to man," as well as to beasts, birds, and creeping things, we frequently recurred to a phrase that has become habitual with me in these later years when other worlds seem anchored close alongside this, and when the telephone, the phonograph, and the microphone begin to show us that every breath carries in itself not only the power, but the scientific certainty of registration: "Well, one thing is certain: we shall meet it in the ether.*"

---

* upper regions of space, i.e., the heavens

One of my companions in the tribulation of learning the bicycle, and the grace of its mastery, was a tall, bright-faced, vigorous-minded young Celt who is devoted to every good word and work and has had much experience with the people of the slums, living among them and trying to build character among those waste places of humanity. I set out to teach this young woman the bicycle, and while she took her lesson—which, as she is young, elastic, and long-limbed, was vastly less difficult than mine—we talked of many things: American women, and why they do not walk; the English lower class, and why they are less vigorous than the Irish; the English girl of the slums, and why she is less self-respecting than an Irish girl in the same station. "There are many things for which we cannot account," said my young friend; whereupon, with the self-elected mentorship of my half-century, I oracularly observed: "Cosmos has not a consequence without a cause; it is the business of reason to seek for causes, and, if it cannot make sure of them, to construct for itself theories as to what they are or will turn out to

At fifty-three I was at more disadvantage than most
people in learning the bicycle, for I suffered from the
sedentary habits of a lifetime.

be when found. But the trouble is, when we have framed our theory, we come to look upon it as our child, that we have brought into the world, nurtured, and trained up by hand. The curse of life is that men will insist on holding their theories as true and imposing them on others; this gives rise to creeds, customs, constitutions, royalties, governments. Happy is he who knows that he knows nothing, or next to nothing, and holds his opinions like a bouquet of flowers in his hand, that sheds its fragrance everywhere, and which he is willing to exchange at any moment for one fairer and more sweet, instead of strapping them on like an armor of steel and thrusting with his lance those who do not accept his notions."

My last teacher was—as ought to be the case on the principle of climax—my best. I think she might have given many a pointer to folks that bring up children, and I realized that no matter how one may think himself accomplished, when he sets out to learn a new language, science, or the bicycle, he has entered a new realm as truly as if he were a child newly born into the world, and "Except ye become as little children" is the law by which he is governed. Whether he will or not he must first creep, then walk, then run; and the wisest guide he can have is the one who most studiously helps him to help himself. This was a truism that I had heard all my life long, but never did a realizing sense of it settle down upon my spirit so thoroughly as when I learned the bicycle. It is not the teacher who holds you in place by main strength that is going to help you win that elusive, reluctant, inevitable prize we call success, but it is the one who, while studiously keeping in the background, steers you to the fore. So Teacher Number 12 had the wit and wisdom to retire to the rear of the saucy steed, that I might form the habit of seeing no sign of aid or comfort from any source except my own reaction on the treadles according to law; yet cunningly contrived, by laying a skilled hand upon the saddle without my observation, knowledge, or consent, to aid me in my balancing. She diminished the weight thus set to my account as rapidly as my own increasing courage and skill rendered this possible.

I have always observed—and not without a certain pleasure, remembering my brother's hardihood—that wherever a woman goes, some man has reached the place before her; and it did not dim the sweetness of my success or the fullness of my content when I had mastered Gladys to ascertain, from a letter sent me by the wife of a man sixty-four years of age who had just learned, that I was "No. 2 " instead of "No. 1," thus obliging me to rectify the frontier of chronology as I had constructed it in relation to the conquest of the bicycle; for I vainly thought that I had fought the antics of Gladys as a sentry on duty away out on the extreme frontier of time.

But at last (which means in two months or thereabouts, at ten or twenty minutes' practice off and on daily) I reached the goal, and could mount the bicycle without the slightest foreign interference or even the moral support of a sympathetic onlooker. In doing this I realized that the totality of what I had learned entered into the action. Every added increment of power that I had gained in balancing, pedaling, steering, taking advantage of the surfaces, adjusting my weight according to my own peculiarities, and so on, was set to my account when I began to manage the bulky steed that behaves worst of all when a novice seeks the saddle and strikes out alone. Just so, I felt, it had been all my life and will be, doubtless, in all worlds and with us all. The totality of native forces and acquired discipline and expert knowledge stands us in good stead for each crisis that we have to meet. There is a momentum, a cumulative power on which we can count in every new circumstance, as a capitalist counts upon his credit at the bank. It is not only a divine declaration, it is one of the basic laws of being, that "all things work together for good."

The one who has learned latest and yet has really learned the mastery of the bicycle is the best teacher. Many a time I have heard boys in college say that it was not the famed mathematician who could teach them anything—he knew too much, he was too far ahead for them to hear his voice, he was impatient of their halting steps—but the tutor who had left college only the year before, and remembering his own

failures and stupidity, had still that fellow-
feeling that made him wondrous kind.

As has been stated, my last epoch consisted of learning to mount; that is the problem
of the whole mathematical undertaking, for
mathematical it is to a nicety. You have to
balance your system more carefully than you
ever did your accounts; not the smallest fraction
can be out of the way, or away you go, the
treacherous steed forming one half of an equa-
tion and yourself with a bruised knee forming
the other. You must add a stroke at just the
right angle to mount, subtract one to descend,
divide them equally to hold your seat, and
multiply all these movements in definite ratio
and true proportion by, the swiftest of all roots,
or you will become the most minus of quantities.
You must foot up your accounts with the
strictest regularity; there can be no partial
payments in a business enterprise like this.

Although I could now mount and descend,
turn corners and get over the ground all by
myself, I still felt a lack of complete faith in
Gladys, although she had never harmed me but

once, and then it was my own fault in letting go the gleaming cross-bar, which is equivalent to dropping the bridle of a spirited steed. Let it be carefully remembered by every beginning bicycler that, whatever she forgets, she must forever keep her "main hold," else her horse is not bitted and will shy to a dead certainty.

As we grew better acquainted I thought how perfectly analogous were our relations to those of friends who became slowly seasoned one to the other: they have endured the vicissitudes of every kind of climate, of the changing seasons; they have known the heavy, water-logged conditions of spring, the shrinkage of summer's trying heat, the happy medium of autumn, and the contracting cold that winter brings; they are like the bits of wood, exactly apportioned and attuned, that go to make up a Stradivarius violin. They can count upon one another and not disagree, because the stress of life has molded them to harmony. They are like the well-worn robe, the easy shoe. There is no short road to this adjustment, so much to be desired; not any will win it short of "patient continuance in well-doing."

I noticed that the great law which I believe to be potential throughout the universe made no exception here: "According to thy faith be it unto thee" was the only law of success. When I felt sure that I should do my pedaling with judicial accuracy, and did not permit myself to dread the swift motion round a bend; when I formed in my mind the image of a successful ascent of the "Priory Rise"; when I fully purposed in my mind that I should not run into the hedge on the one side or the iron fence on the other, these prophecies were fulfilled with practical certainty. I fell into the habit of varying my experience by placing before myself the image—so germane to the work in which I am engaged—of an inebriate in action with the accompanying mental panorama of reeling to and fro and staggering like a drunken man; but I could never go through this three consecutive times without lurching off the saddle. But when I put before me, as distinctly as my powers of concentration would permit, the image of my mother holding steadily above me a pair of balances, and looking at me with that quizzical expectant glance I knew so well, and saying: "Do it? Of course you'll do it; what else should you do?" I found that it was palpably helpful in enabling me to "sit straight and hold my own" on my uncertain steed. She always maintained, in the long talks we had concerning immortality, that the law I mention was conclusive, and was wont to close our conversations on that subject (in which I held the interrogative position) with some such remark as this: "If Professor _____ thinks he is not immortal he probably is not; if I think I am I may be sure I shall be, for is it not written in the law, 'According to thy faith be it unto thee'?"

Gradually I realized a consoling degree of mastery over Gladys; but nothing was more apparent to me than that we were not yet thoroughly acquainted—we had not summered and wintered together. I had not learned her kinks, and she was as full of them as the most spirited mare that sweeps the course on a Kentucky race-track. Although I have seen a race but once (and that was in the Champs Elysées, Paris, a quarter of a century ago), I am yet so much interested in the fact that it is a Flora Temple, a Goldsmith Maid, a Maud S., a Sunol, a California Maid that often stands first on the record, that I would fain have named my shying steed after one of these; but as she was a gift from Lady Henry Somerset, this seemed invidious in me as a Yankee woman, and so I called her Gladys, having in view the bright spirit of the donor, the exhilarating motion of the machine, and the gladdening effect of its acquaintance and use on my health and disposition.

As I have said, I found from first to last that the process of acquisition exactly coincided with that which had given me everything I possessed of physical, mental, or moral success— that is, skill, knowledge, character. I was learning the bicycle precisely as I learned the a-b-c. When I set myself, as a stint, to mount and descend in regular succession anywhere from twenty to fifty times, it was on the principle that we do a thing more easily the second time than the first, the third time than the second, and so on in a rapidly increasing ratio, until it is done without any conscious effort whatever. This was precisely the way in which my mother trained me to tell the truth, and my music teacher taught me that mastership of the piano keyboard (which I have lost by disuse). Falling from grace may mean falling from a habit formed—how do we know? This opens a boundless field of ethical speculation which I would gladly have followed, but just then the steel steed gave a lurch as if to say, "Tend to your knitting"—the favorite expression of a Rocky Mountain stage driver when tourists taxed him with questions while he was turning round a bend two thousand feet above the valley.

And now comes the question "What do the doctors say?" Here follow several testimonies:

"The question now of great interest to girls is in regard to the healthfulness of the wheel. Many are prophesying dire results from this fascinating exercise, and fond parents are refusing to allow their daughters to ride because they are girls. It will be a delight to girls to learn that the fact of their sex is, in itself, not a bar to riding a wheel. If the girl is normally constituted and is dressed hygienically, and if she will use judgment and not overtax herself in learning to ride, and in measuring the length of rides after she has learned, she is in no more danger from riding a wheel than is the young man. But if she persists in riding in a tight dress, and uses no judgment in deciding the amount of exercise she is capable of safely taking, it will be quite possible for her to injure herself, and then it is she, and not the wheel, that is to blame. Many physicians are now coming to regard the 'wheel' as beneficial to the health of women as well as of men."

Dr. Seneca Egbert says: "As an exercise bicycling is superior to most, if not all, others at our command. It takes one into the outdoor air; it is entirely under control; can be made gentle or vigorous as one desires; is active and not passive; takes the rider outside of himself and the thoughts and cares of his daily work; develops his will, his attention, his courage and independence; and makes pleasant what is otherwise most irksome. Moreover, the exercise is well and equally distributed over almost the whole body, and when all the muscles are exercised, no muscle is likely to be over-exercised."

He advocates cycling as a remedy for dyspepsia, torpid liver, incipient consumption, nervous exhaustion, rheumatism, and melancholia. In regard to the exercise for women he says: "It gets them out of doors, gives them a form of exercise adapted to their needs, one that they may enjoy in company with others or alone and that goes to the root of their nervous troubles."

He instances two cases, of girls fourteen and eighteen years of age, where a decided increase in height could be fairly attributed to cycling.

The question is often asked if riding a wheel is not the same as running a sewing-machine. Let the same doctor answer: "Not at all. Women, at least, sit erect on a wheel, and consequently the thighs never make even a right angle with the trunk, and there is no stasis of blood in the lower limbs and genitalia. Moreover, the work itself makes the rider breathe in oceans of fresh air; while the woman at the sewing-machine works indoors, stoops over her work, contracting the chest and almost completely checking the flow of blood to and from the lower half of her body, where at the same time she is increasing the demand for it, finally aggravating the whole trouble by the pressure of the lower edge of the corset against the abdomen, so that the customary congestions and displacements have good cause for their existence."

"The great desideratum in all recreations is pure air, plenty of it, and lungs free to absorb it." (Dr. Lyman B. Sperry)

"Let go, but stand by"—this is the golden rule for parent and pastor, teacher and friend; the only rule that at once respects the individuality of another and yet adds one's own, so far as may be, to another's momentum in the struggle of life.

How difficult it is for the trainer to judge exactly how much force to exercise in helping to steer the wheel and start the wheeler along the highway! In this the point of view makes all the difference. The trainer is tall, the rider short; the first can poise on the off-treadle while one foot is on the ground, but the last must learn to balance while one foot is in the air. For one of these perfectly to comprehend the other's relation to the vehicle is practically impossible; the degree to which he may attain this depends upon the amount of imagination to the square inch with which he has been fitted out. The opacity of the mind, its inability to project itself into the realm of another's personality, goes a long way to explain the friction of life. If we would set down other people's errors to this rather than to malice prepense we should not only get more good out of life and feel more kindly toward our fellows, but doubtless the rectitude of our intellects would increase, and the justice of our judgments. For instance, it is my purpose, so far as I understand myself, to be considerate toward those about me; but my pursuits have been almost purely mental, and to perceive what would seem just to one whose pursuits have been almost purely mechanical would require an act of imagination of which I am wholly incapable. We are so shut away from one another that none tells those about him what he considers ideal treatment on their part toward him. He thinks about it all the same, mumbles about it to himself, mutters about it to those of his own guild, and these mutterings make the discontent that finally breaks out in reforms whose tendency is to distribute the good things of this life more equally among the living. But nothing will probe to the core of this the greatest disadvantage under which we labor—that is, mutual non-comprehension—except a basis of society and government which would make it easy for each to put himself in another's place because his place is so much like another's. We shall be less imaginative, perhaps, in those days—the critics say this is inevitable; but it will only be because we need less imagination in order to do that which is just and kind to every one about us.

In my early home my father always set us children to work by stints—that is, he measured off a certain part of the garden to be weeded, or other work to be done, and when we had accomplished it our working hours were over.

With this deeply ingrained habit in full force I set myself stints with the bicycle. In the later part of my novitiate fifty attempts a day were allotted to that most difficult of all achievements, learning to mount, and I calculate that five hundred such efforts well put in will solve that most intricate problem of specific gravity.

Now concerning falls: I set out with the determination not to have any. Though mentally adventurous I have always been physically cautious; a student of physiology in my youth, I knew the reason why I brought so much less elasticity to my task than did my young and agile trainers. I knew the penalty of broken bones, for these a tricycle had cost me some years before. My trainers were kind enough to encourage me by saying that if I became an expert in slow riding I should take the rapid wheel as a matter of course and thus be really more accomplished (in the long run as well as the short) than by any other process. So I have had but one real downfall to record as the result of my three months' practice, and it illustrates the old saying that "pride goeth before destruc-

tion, and a haughty spirit before a fall;" for I
was not a little lifted up by having learned to
dismount with confidence and ease—I will not
say with grace, for at fifty-three that would be
an affectation—so one bright morning I bowled
on down the Priory drive waving my hand to
my most adventurous aide-de-camp, and calling
out as I left her behind, "Now you will see how
nicely I can do it—watch!" when behold! that
timid left foot turned traitor, and I came down
solidly on my knee, and the knee on a pebble
as relentless as prejudice and as opinionated
as ignorance. The nervous shock made me
well-nigh faint, the bicycle tumbled over on
my prone figure, and I wished I had never
heard of Gladys or of any wheel save "ye wheels
of time."

Let me remark to any young woman who
reads this page that for her to tumble off her
bike is inexcusable. The lightsome elasticity
of every muscle, the quickness of the eye, the
agility of motion, ought to preserve her from
such a catastrophe. I have had no more falls
simply because I would not. I have proceeded

on a basis of the utmost caution, and aside
from that one pitiful performance the bicycle
has cost me hardly a single bruise.

Ethereal Episode

They that know nothing fear nothing.
Away back in 1886 my alert young friend and
assistant, Miss Anna Gordon,[3] and my ingenious young niece, Miss Katharine Willard, took
to the tricycle as naturally as ducks take to
water. The very first time they mounted they
went spinning down the long shady street, with
its pleasant elms, in front of Rest Cottage,
where for nearly a generation mother and I had
had our home. Even as the war-horse snuffeth
the battle from afar, I longed to go and do
likewise. Remembering my country bringing-up
and various exploits in running, climbing and

horseback riding, I said to myself, "If those girls can ride without learning so can I!" Taking out my watch I timed them as they, at my suggestion, set out to make a record in going round the square. Two and a half minutes was the result. I then started with all my forces well in hand, and flew around in two and a quarter minutes. Not contented with this, but puffed up with foolish vanity, I declared that I would go around in two minutes; and, encouraged by their cheers, away I went without a fear till the third turning-post was reached, when the left hand played me false, and turning at an acute angle, away I went sidelong, machine and all, into the gutter, falling on my right elbow, which felt like a glassful of chopped ice, and I knew that for the first time in a life full of vicissitudes I had been really hurt. Anna Gordon's white face as she ran toward me caused me to wave my uninjured hand and call out "Never mind!" and with her help I rose and walked into the house, wishing above all things to go straight to my own room and lie on my own bed, and thinking as I did so how pathetic is that instinct that makes "the stricken deer go weep," and the harmed hare seek the covert.

Two physicians were soon at my side, and my mother, then over eighty years of age, came in with much controlled agitation and seated herself beside my bed, taking my hand and saying, "O Frank! you were always too adventurous."

Our family physician was out of town, and the two gentlemen were well-nigh strangers. It was a kind face, that of the tall, thin man who looked down upon me in my humiliation, put his ear against my heart to see if there would be any harm in administering ether, handled my elbow with a woman's gentleness, and then said to his assistant "Now let us begin." And to me who had been always well, and knew nothing of such unnatural proceedings, he remarked, "Breathe into the funnel—full, natural breaths; that is all you have to do."

I set myself to my task, as has been my wont always, and soon my mother and my friend, Anna Gordon, who were fanning me with big "palm-leaves," became grotesque and then ridiculous, and I remember saying, "You are a couple of enormous crickets standing on your hind legs, and you have each a spear of dry grass, and you look as if you were paralyzed; and you wave your withered spears of grass, and you call that fanning a poor woman who is suffocating before your eyes." I labored with them, entreated them, and dealt with them in great plainness—so much so that my mother could not bear to hear me talk in such a foolish fashion, and quietly withdrew to her own room, closed the door, and sat down to possess her soul in patience until the operation should be over.

Then the scene changed, and as they put on the splints pain was involved, and I heard those about me laughing in the most unfeeling manner while I murmured: "She always believed in humanity—she always said she did and would; and she has lived in this town thirty years, and they are hurting her—they are hurting her dreadfully; and if they keep on she will lose her faith in human nature, and if she should it will be the greatest calamity that can happen to a human being."

Now the scene changed once more—I was in the starry heavens, and said to the young friends who had come in and stood beside me: "Here are stars as thick as apples on a bough, and if you are good you shall each have one. And, Anna, because you are good, and always have been, you shall be given a whole solar system to manage just as you like. The Heavenly Father has no end of them; He tosses them out of His hand as a boy does marbles; He spins them like a cocoon; He has just as many after He has given them away as He had before He began."

Then there settled down upon me the most vivid and pervading sense of the love of God that I have ever known. I can give no adequate conception of it, and what I said, as my comrades repeated it to me, was something after this order:

"We are like blood-drops floating through the great heart of our Heavenly Father. We are infinitely safe, and cared for as tenderly as a baby in its mother's arms. No harm can come anywhere near us; what we call harm will turn out to be the very best and kindest way of leading us to be our best selves. There is no terror in the universe, for God is always at the center of everything. He is love, as we read in the good book, and He has but one wish—that we should love one another; in Him we live, and move, and have our being."

Little by little, freeing my mind of all sorts of queer notions, I came back out of the only experience of the kind that I have ever known; but I must say that had I not learned the great evils that result from using anesthetics I should have wished to try ether again, just for the ethical and spiritual help that came to me. It let me out into a new world, greater, more mellow, more godlike, and it did me no harm at all.

In Conclusion

f I am asked to explain why I learned the bicycle, I should say I did it as an act of grace, if not of actual religion. The cardinal doctrine laid down by my physician was, "Live out of doors and take congenial exercise;" but from the day when, at sixteen years of age, I was enwrapped in the long skirts that impeded every footstep, I have detested walking and felt with a certain noble disdain that the conventions of life had cut me off from what in the freedom of my prairie home had been one of life's sweetest joys. Driving is not real exercise; it does not renovate the river of blood that flows so sluggishly in the veins of those who from any cause have lost the natural adjustment of brain to brawn. Horseback riding, which does promise vigorous exercise, is expensive. The bicycle, however, meets all the conditions and will ere long come within the reach of all. Therefore, in obedience to the laws of health, I learned to ride. I also wanted to help women to a wider world, for I hold that the more interests women and men can have in common, in thought, word, and deed, the happier will it be for the home. Besides, there was a special value to women in the conquest of the bicycle by a woman in her fifty-third year, and one who had so many comrades in the white-ribbon army of temperance workers[4] that her action would be widely influential. Then there were three minor reasons:

I did it from pure natural love of adventure—a love long hampered and impeded, like a brook that runs underground, but in this enterprise bubbling up again with somewhat of its pristine freshness and taking its merry course as of old.

Second, from a love of acquiring this new implement of power and literally putting it underfoot.

Last, but not least, because a good many people thought I could not do it at my age.

It is needless to say that a bicycling costume was a prerequisite. This consisted of a skirt and blouse of tweed, with belt, rolling collar, and loose cravat, the skirt three inches from the ground; a round straw hat, and walking shoes with gaiters. It was a simple, modest suit, to which no person of common sense could take exception.

As nearly as I can make out, reducing the problem to actual figures, it took me about three months, with an average of fifteen minutes' practice daily, to learn, first, to pedal; second, to turn; third, to dismount; and fourth, to mount independently this most mysterious animal. January 20th will always be a red-letter bicycle day, because although I had already mounted several times with no hand on the rudder, some good friend had always stood by to lend moral support; but summoning all my force, on this day, I mounted and started off alone. From that hour the spell was broken; Gladys was no more a mystery: I had learned all her kinks, had put a bridle in her teeth, and touched her smartly with the whip of victory. Consider, ye who are of a considerable chronology: in about thirteen hundred minutes, or, to put it more mildly, in twenty-two hours, or, to put it most mildly of all, in less than a single day as the almanac reckons time—but practically in two days of actual practice—amid the delightful surroundings of the great outdoors, and inspired by the bird-songs, the color and fragrance of an English posy-garden, in the company of devoted and pleasant comrades, I had made myself master of the most remarkable, ingenious, and inspiring motor ever yet devised upon this planet.

Moral: Go thou and do likewise!

Notes

1. Rest Cottage, in Evanston, Illinois, was built by Willard's family in 1866 and was her home for the remainder of her life. From her office there, she directed the Woman's Christian Temperance Union. She was president of the national organization from 1879 to her death in 1898. Rest Cottage is now the Frances Willard Museum, and Willard's bicycle, Gladys, is on display. The home is part of the present-day National WCTU headquarters.

2. Lady Henry Somerset was president of the British Woman's Temperance Association. She and Willard met at the first World WCTU convention in 1891 and developed a close personal friendship. During the years 1892 to 1896, Willard spent most of her time in England at the homes of Lady Henry—Eastnor Castle and the Priory at Reigate Manor. She received generous financial support (as well as the gift of her bicycle) from Lady Henry.

3. Anna Gordon was Willard's "devoted friend, faithful secretary, and constant travelling companion" for twenty years, acting as personal aide and confidant. Without her efficiency, organization, and emotional support, Willard's work would never have been as effective. After Frances' death in 1898, Gordon wrote two Willard biographies. Gordon, herself, was president of the WCTU from 1914 to 1925 and saw temperance hopes finally realized in the Eighteenth Amendment.

4. The white ribbon was the symbol of the Woman's Christian Temperance Union.

Women and Cycling:
The Early Years

by Lisa Larrabee

Frances Willard was not the first woman to
discover the sense of freedom and thrill of accomplishment bicycling could bring. As early as 1819,
engravings of women astride draisiennes (forerunners
of the bicycle) were made. The first recorded ride by
a woman on a pedal-driven bicycle occurred in 1842
in Scotland when Mary Marchbank, niece of bicycle
inventor Kirkpatrick Macmillan, took a ride on one
of her uncle's machines. Twenty-six years later, the
first women's bicycle race was held in Bordeaux,
France on November 1, 1868. The following year, at
least five women entered the first known bicycle road
race, an 83-mile ride from from Paris to Rouen. In
most countries, though, racing remained a risqué
activity for females throughout the nineteenth
century.

Aside from these early enthusiasts, few women
rode bicycles, and it was for a very good reason. The
most popular bicycle, up until around 1885, was the
"ordinary" or "penny-farthing," as the English called

it (the size of its large front wheel compared to the very small back wheel reminded them of a penny as compared to the quarter-cent farthing). Although the size of the front wheel made the direct pedal-drive more efficient, it was very common to fly over the huge front wheel when the bicycle bumped into anything. Thus, few women attempted the ordinaries.

THE BICYCLE OF 1879.

In the 1880's, many English riders adopted the much safer tricycle. The upper-class thought tricycling to be more dignified than bicycling and consigned the latter to the lower-classes, sometimes even shunning the use of roads frequented by two-wheelers. Tricycling made fewer demands than bicycling and was more appealing to the older generation and to women used to thinking of themselves as physically inferior.

Tricycles were also more expensive than bicycles, providing a further element of snobbery. Included among the fans of this type of transportation was Queen Victoria, who had two tricycles specially made by James Starley and delivered to the royal residence in 1881. Whether or not the Queen ever mounted her machines is not known, but her purchase of them endorsed the use of the tricycle by women. Consequently, the number of female riders in England soared. Tricycling was viewed as an acceptable feminine activity, since it allowed riders to wear skirts with reasonable comfort and propriety.

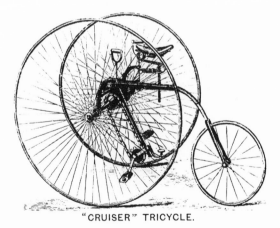

"CRUISER" TRICYCLE.

In the United States, tricycling never caught on among women, and only a few attempted it. If a woman did go tricycling, *The Wheelman* magazine advised her to find a male cyclist to ride along with her: "In this way the lady learns with ease; she is provided with a suitable escort; and if anything goes wrong, she has assistance at hand." Women who tricycled without male escorts were often the victims of verbal harassment from pedestrians.

The decade of the 1880's brought the "safety" bicycle, the direct forerunner of the modern-day machine. Because the wheels of the chain-driven safety bicycle were nearly equivalent in size, it was far easier to ride than the ordinary and quickly gained immense world-wide popularity among both women and men, upper-class and working class.

The first mass production of women's safety bicycles came in 1889, when the Starley Brothers introduced the "Psycho Ladies' Bicycle." As the bicycling craze intensified, almost every company produced one or more special models for the women who made up nearly one third of their market. Early manufacturers often used much of their advertising space to show why bicycles could be ridden by respectable ladies; in other words, how women could retain their femininity while astride two wheels.

Among the many accessories especially for women was the Cherry's Screen, invented by West Virginian Theron Cherry. This device blocked the view of a lady's ankles and feet, and also prevented her skirt from blowing about. Attached to the front of the bicycle, it looked something like large bat wings. Another company offered an all-black "mourning" bicycle in an attempt to tap the widow market.

Health and the Bicycle

Because the issue of whether women should ride bicycles was so emotionally charged in the 1880's and 1890's, debates over the medicinal benefits of bicycling, or lack of them, became especially heated when women were concerned. *The Idler* quotes one doctor as proclaiming that bicycling was "good for girls, but bad for women." Even when doctors did approve of women cyclists, they usually said women should practice moderation in their efforts. In the words of Dr. J. West Roosevelt from an 1895 *Scribner's*, "There is no reason to think that a healthy woman can be injured by using the wheel" on the condition that "she does not over-exert herself by riding too long a time, or too fast, or up too steep hills." Arguing against bicycling for women, one Parisian claimed that bicycling ruined the "feminine organs of matrimonial necessity," thus bringing about the end of womanhood. It was also claimed that bicycling would destroy "feminine symmetry and poise," as women would develop muscular legs, which would be an unsightly contrast to undeveloped "feminine" arms. Some feared bicycling would affect pelvic muscles and increase the labor pains of childbirth. Another possible malady was "bicycle eye," caused by prolonged raising of the eyes while the head was lowered in a riding position.

On the other side of the debate, many doctors argued for women bicyclists, including one New Yorker who claimed that bicycling had arrived just in time to save women from remaining housebound and "being morbid." An 1896 *Harper's Bazar* trumpeted the benefits of the pastime as not only bestowing "on every cheek a natural bloom, lips that are indeed 'cherry ripe,' arms rounded and muscular, limbs straight and strong," but also "a healthy tone to the voice, a sparkle in the eye, and an unshackled freedom of manner." In the same year, after listing in *The Forum* a full page of the health benefits female cyclists enjoyed, writer Henry J. Garrigues added, "In women it is apt to overcome the impulsiveness and whimsicality which render many of them unhappy." Another writer argued in an 1895 issue of *The Cosmopolitan* that by riding a bicycle, a woman would "become mistress of herself," transformed into "a rational, useful being restored to health and sanity."

Some doctors believed that cycling would allow women to throw off the bondage of corsets. By tightly constricting a woman's body, the corset made a woman appear to have an hour glass-shaped figure. Although required by the fashions of the day, corsets sometimes caused fainting and could endanger pregnant women and their unborn children. Many women cited this risk when they argued for "rational dress," practical clothing without corsets. A writer for the *Lady Cyclist* had harsh words for what some physicians called "the murderous corset":

Nothing short of death seems to make the apathetic woman of fashion recognize that her life is one long suicide. Hers is a living death; fainting, hysteria, indigestion, anaemia, lassitude, diminished vitality and a host of other sufferings arise from interference with the circulation of the blood and the prevention of the full play of the breathing organs. Such is the woman of old, now happily dying out. Dress reform is one of the great factors in this result, and the cycle is an aid to this reform.

RIDING OR BICYCLING CORSET.

A New Emancipation

Whether or not they were freed from their corsets, women bicyclists had the opportunity to be freed from chaperones, and others who might interfere with their newfound liberty. In 1895 one woman observed in *Scribner's*: "No outdoor pastime can be more independently pursued." The chief concern of those morally against women riding bicycles centered on the belief that women would become wild and wicked if left unchaperoned. And most elderly chaperones found it too difficult to keep up with speedy young cyclists.

One American writer, quoted in James McGurn's history of cycling, claimed that the "unfettered liberty" of bicycling would "intoxicate" women to immoral acts. Others argued that bicycling was the number one reason for an increase in the "ranks of reckless girls who became outcast women." Many critics believed that bicycle seats were shaped in such a way as might stimulate a woman's sexual excitement. Influenced by these beliefs, some people lobbied to have bicycling outlawed for females. One southern city in the United States actually banned female cyclists from its streets.

The arguments over women riding bicycles echoed a larger concern during the fading Victorian era—that women were losing their femininity. In his book on bicycling history, Seamus McGonagle cites the following as a typical complaint: "At least half the interest of one sex in the other arises from their respective dependent and protective positions. When a lady velocipedes she destroys all this kind of subtle interest." Other accusations hurled at female bicyclists included portrayals of them as masculine, indecent, and home-wrecking.

At least one voice of reason, however, pointed out that many things that had once been considered "fast and unfeminine" had become part of "the ordinary programme of a woman's life," and that bicycling would probably follow their example. The magazine *Scribner's* reported that "the occasional denunciation of the pastime as unwomanly is fortunately lost in the general approval that a new and wholesome recreation has been found." Frances Willard even discovered "high moral uses in the bicycle and [could] commend it as a teacher without pulpit or creed."

Regardless of the morality issue, one thing was certain—the bicycle was viewed by many women as a "freedom machine." Susan B. Anthony, pioneer in the struggle for women's rights, believed that bicycling did "more to emancipate woman than anything else in the world." She added that bicycling gave women "a feeling of freedom and self-reliance," and that, "the moment she takes her seat she knows she can't get into harm unless she gets off her bicycle." A woman awheel, Anthony believed, was "the picture of free, untrammelled womanhood." Bicycles liberated many women from domesticity and isolation, and contributed to their struggle to gain a foothold on something closer to equality than the Victorian era had previously offered.

A few ideas, however, were a bit too radical to find acceptance in the 1890's. Belva Lockwood, one of the most important female attorneys in the United States, proposed women bicyclists as press correspondents for the front lines in war. In 1895, Ann Strong declared in the *Minneapolis Tribune* that bicycles were "just as good company as most husbands" and that when a bicycle gets shabby or old a woman could "dispose of it and get a new one without shocking the entire community." Men generally did not appreciate Miss Strong's attitude, and one man wrote some verse expressing his exasperation:

> *I clasped the waist of fair Lenore,*
> *I praised her matchless worth,*
> *And asked her if she loved me more*
> *Than all else on earth.*
> *She nestled closer to my side,*
> *I thrilled from head to heel*
> *As she in whispered words replied*
> *"Yes dear — except my wheel."*

One young American woman, Margaret Valentine Le Long, took her freedom to the limit when, in 1896, she rode, *alone*, more than half-way across the United States. Le Long ignored the objections of her relatives and friends, and set out on her amazing two-month journey from Chicago to San Francisco. (In contrast, it took Elaine Mariolle just over ten days to ride her bicycle all the way across the United States in a 1986 race.) Margaret followed railroad tracks through Nebraska, Wyoming, Utah, Nevada, and California to reach her destination in San Francisco. She carried a light load—a skirt, change of underwear, clean hanky, toilet articles, and a pistol. She only had to use her gun once, and that was to scatter a herd of unmoving cattle in Wyoming. She felt that she had not been bothered by tramps, cowboys, or Indians because she had worn a skirt and not "unladylike bloomers."

Clothing Reform and Beyond

Before bloomers became popular wear for women bicyclists, *Outing* magazine presented a column by Grace Denison in which she recommended modes of dress for female cyclists. This 1892 column was short-lived but did provide helpful hints, such as ways to keep one's skirt from flying about. These methods included sewing lead weights into hems and using leather-lined skirts. Denison also advocated slightly shortened skirts, which she felt would help prevent entanglements with bicycle parts and allow easier movement. Despite these and other suggestions, long skirts continued to hinder women bicyclists from efficient pedaling, interfered with their balance, and endangered women riders by becoming tangled in the bicycle.

Although bloomers had existed since 1848, it took nearly forty years before the first bloomer-clad women were seen riding bicycles in the United States. Bloomers were invented in the Oneida Community of New York and named for Amelia Bloomer, editor of *Lily* magazine, who popularized their use during the 1850's in the United States. After a lull of thirty years, they again became fashionable attire when their appropriateness for riding the safety bicycle was realized, and soon they were a central part of the rational dress movement. While women who rode tricycles could easily do so while wearing skirts, the feat of riding a bicycle was more safely and gracefully accomplished while wearing bloomers. In 1894 Albert Pope started using bloomer-clad women in his advertisements, and within a year, bloomers were commonly seen on women cyclists throughout the United States.

Some American bicycle clubs held dances exclusively for bloomer-clad women and their partners. But not everyone approved of the new costume. In 1895, after a successful bloomer dance, police in Chicago put a stop to these events by threatening to treat women in bloomers like prostitutes. A Chicago woman was actually fined twenty-five dollars for wearing such an unladylike garment. In Norwich, New York, a group of male objectors formed an Anti-Bloomer Brigade, taking an oath to avoid associating with women in bloomers. Many smaller American communities were successful in preventing bloomer-clad women from bicycling on their streets, or appearing anywhere else. One young church organist was threatened with excommunication after she wore bright red bloomers in church!

Elizabeth Cady Stanton defended bloomers, and believed that women should be granted the freedom to choose what they would wear. Other proponents pointed out that low-cut ball gowns and bathing costumes, both of which were socially acceptable, were far more revealing than bloomers.

A compromise garment of a half-skirt, half-bloomer was even created. The bicyclist could, with a series of drawstrings, make her skirt into bloomers for riding her bicycle, and then, by releasing the drawstrings, recreate the skirt. This ingenious invention helped lessen the tension for both sides during a period of radical change. Finally in 1895, at the height of the bicycle's world-wide popularity, upper-class American women endorsed the wearing of bloomers, thus paving the way for more wide-spread acceptance. Even though the bloomer fad was over by 1898, the clothing reform that went along with it saw the near riddance of corsets and the first sight of women's ankles and calves.

The clothes inspired by women on bicycles had helped lead the way to independence and reform. Frances Willard had predicted that if women dressed rationally while riding, "many prejudices as to what they may be allowed to wear would melt away." It was the judgment of one writer in *The Cosmopolitan* that, in terms of dress reform: "What years of eloquent preaching from the platforms of woman's suffrage" had failed to accomplish, "the necessities of the bicycle had in a few months brought into practical use." As Robert Smith has pointed out:

> *In all probability the most lasting social consequence of the bicycle craze was the effect it had on American women . . . The drive to wear "rational dress" in the 1890's . . . was a much greater blow in behalf of the emancipation of women than taking off a brassiere.*

One of the most encompassing summaries of the bicycle's role in the eventual demise of the Victorian woman was provided by the English novelist and playwright, John Galsworthy. Having witnessed firsthand the bicycle craze of the 1890's, Galsworthy wrote:

> *The bicycle . . . has been responsible for more movement in manners and morals than anything since Charles the Second. Under its influence, wholly or it part, have wilted*

chaperons, long and narrow skirts, tight corsets, hair that would come down, black stockings, thick ankles, large hats, prudery and fear of the dark; under its influence, wholly or in part, have bloomed weekends, strong nerves, strong legs, strong language, knickers, knowledge of make and shape, knowledge of woods and pastures, equality of sex, good digestion and professional occupation — in four words, the emancipation of women.

Bibliography

Frances Willard

Blocker, Jack S., Jr. "Progressivism Anticipated: Temperance Women, Home Protection and Women's Rights, 1873-1933." Conference on Women in the Progressive Era, National Museum of American History, Smithsonian Institution, March 1988. In press: University of Kentucky Press.

———. *Retreat from Reform: The Prohibition Movement in the United States, 1890-1913.* Westport, CT: Greenwood Press, 1976.

Bordin, Ruth. *Frances Willard: A Biography.* Chapel Hill: University of North Carolina Press, 1986.

———. *Woman and Temperance: The Quest for Power and Liberty, 1873-1900.* Philadelphia: Temple University Press, 1981.

Earhart, Mary (Dillon). *Frances Willard: From Prayers to Politics.* Chicago: University of Chicago Press, 1944.

Gordon, Anna A. *The Beautiful Life of Frances Willard.* Chicago: Woman's Temperance Publishing Association, 1898.

Gordon, Elizabeth Putnam. *Women Torchbearers: The Story of the Woman's Christian Temperance Union.* Evanston, IL: Woman's Temperance Publishing Association, 1924.

Hays, Agnes Dubbs. *Heritage of Dedication: One Hundred Years of the National Woman's Christian Temperance Union, 1874-1974.* Evanston, IL: Signal Press, 1973.

Willard, Frances. *Glimpses of Fifty Years: The Biography of an American Woman* [1839-1889]. Chicago: Woman's Temperance Publishing Association, 1889. Republished New York: Source Book Press, 1970.

Women and Cycling

Articles

"The American Velocipede." *Harper's Weekly* (Dec. 19, 1868): p. 811.

"The Country Club." *Harper's Bazar* (Oct. 3, 1896): p. 827.

"The Etiquette of the Road." *Harper's Weekly* (Oct. 3, 1896): pp. 973-4.

"Ladies 'On the Road.'" *All the Year* 73 (July 29, 1893): pp. 105-09.

Bishop, Joseph B. "Social and Economic Influence of the Bicycle." *The Forum* (Aug. 1896): pp. 680-89.

Cushing, Harry A. "The Moderns Awheel." *Harper's Weekly* (April 11, 1896): p. 353.

de Koven, Mrs. Reginald. "Bicycling for Women." *The Cosmopolitan* 19.4 (Aug. 1895): pp. 386-94.

Freifeld, Karen, and Sheldon Engelmay. "Easy Rider." *Health* 16 (Feb. 1984): pp. 21-4.

Garrigues, Henry J. "Woman and the Bicycle." *The Forum* (Jan. 1896): pp. 578-87.

Greene, Millie S. "A Cycling Courtship." *Belgravia* (1897): pp. 86-101.

Hubert, Philip G., Jr. "The Bicycle: The Wheel of Today." *Scribner's Magazine* 17.6 (June 1895): pp. 692-702.

Humphry, Mrs. "Women on Wheels." *The Idler* 8 (Aug. 1895 - Jan. 1896): pp. 71-74.

Merington, Marguerite. "Woman and the Bicycle." *Scribner's Magazine* 17.6 (June 1895): pp. 702-04.

Mitchell, Barbara J. "When the Wheels Began To Turn." *Women's Sports & Fitness* 9 (March 1987): p. 14.

Russak, Renee. "Women on Wheels." *Bicycling* 29 (June 1988): pp. 56-61.

Richardson, Dr. B.W. "How Cycling Injures Health." *Review of Reviews* (April 1890): pp. 287-88.

Roosevelt, Dr. J. West. "A Doctor's View of Bicycling." *Scribner's Magazine* 17.6 (June 1895): pp. 708-13.

Shenker, Sandy. "Swell on Wheels." *Ms.* 3 (July 1974): pp. 44-5.

Simpson, Jerry H., Jr. "Murphy's Marvelous Mile." *American History Illustrated* 15 (June 1980): 22-33.

Sorensen, Susan. "Evolution of a Dream: From Da Vinci to Daedalus." *Bicycling* 29 (Dec. 1988): 68-74.

Townsend, James B. "Cycle Touring." *Harper's Weekly* (April 11, 1896): p. 354.

———. "The Social Side of Bicycling." *Scribner's Magazine* 17.6 (June 1895): pp. 704-08.

Williams, Dr. Henry Smith. "The Bicycle in Relation to Health." *Harper's Weekly* (April 11, 1896): p. 370.

Books

Alderson, Frederick. *Bicycling: A History.* New York: Praeger Publishers, 1972.

Baranet, Nancy Neiman. *Bicycling: The Bicycle in Recreation, Competition, Transportation.* New York: A.S. Barnes and Company, 1973.

Bicycling eds. *Cycling for Women.* Emmaus, PA: Rodale Press, 1989.

Calif, Ruth. *The World on Wheels: An Illustrated History of the Bicycle and Its Relatives*. New York: Cornwall Books, 1983.

Galsworthy, John. *On Forsyte 'Change*. New York: Charles Scribner's Sons, 1920, 1930.

Leonard, Irving A. *When Bikehood Was in Flower*. South Tamworth, NH: Bearcamp Press, 1969.

Mariolle, Elaine, and Michael Shermer. *The Woman Cyclist*. Chicago: Contemporary Books, 1988.

McGonagle, Seamus. *The Bicycle in Life, Love, War, and Literature*. London: Pelham Books, 1968.

McGowan, Joseph. *History of the Sacramento Valley*. Vol. II. New York: Lewis Historical Publishing Co., 1961, pp. 59-68.

McGurn, James. *On Your Bicycle: An Illustrated History of Cycling*. New York: Facts On File Publications, 1987.

Ritchie, Andrew. *King of the Road*. London: Wildwood House, 1975.

Robertson, Patrick. *The Book of Firsts*. New York: Bramhall House, 1982, pp. 40-43, 244-46, 433.

Rochlin, Jay and Gail, eds. *The Art of "The Wheelman."* Tucson, AZ: Seven Palms Press, 1982.

Russell, Alan, et al., eds. *1988 Guiness Book of World Records*. New York: Sterling Publishing Co., Inc., 1988, pp. 361-62.

Smith, Robert A. *A Social History of The Bicycle*. New York: American Heritage Press, 1972.

Wells, H.G. *The Wheels of Chance*. London: Dent, 1896.

Wilcockson, John. *Bicycle*. New York: Butterick Publishing, 1980.

Woloch, Nancy. *Women and the American Experience*. New York: A.A. Knopf, 1984.

Woodforde, John. *The Story of the Bicycle*. New York: Universe Books, 1970.

About the Authors

Frances Willard (1839-1898) was widely known in the United States and abroad for her social reform efforts. Her causes included temperance, women's suffrage and education, eight hour workday, prison reform, and public kindergarten. She served as president of the Woman's Christian Temperance Union from 1879 until her death in 1898, building it into the largest women's organization of its time. She also founded the World WCTU, the first international organization of women. She was a popular and prolific writer, and her account of learning to ride the bicycle was a best-selling book when originally published in 1895 as *A Wheel Within a Wheel*. Her home in Evanston, Illinois, is now the Frances E. Willard Museum, where her bicycle "Gladys" is on display.

Edith Mayo ("Do Everything": The Life and Work of Frances Willard) is Curator of Political History, National Museum of American History, Smithsonian Institution, Washington, DC.

Lisa Larrabee (Women and Cycling: The Early Years) is the editor of the history and science quarterly, *Interchange*, and has served as guest curator at the Sacramento (California) History Museum.

Acknowledgements

How I Learned to Ride the Bicycle is the result of the assistance and support of many people and organizations. I first learned of Frances Willard's 1895 book from Helaine Victoria Press, publisher of postcards depicting women in history. Rachel Kelly and the National Woman's Christian Temperance Union provided me with an original copy of *A Wheel Within a Wheel*. Edith Mayo's introduction, "Do Everything," adds greatly to an understanding of Willard and her role in the nineteenth century women's reform movement. Lisa Larrabee extensively researched and wrote the fascinating history of women and cycling. Kathleen Hallam did the major tasks of editing and rewriting. I relied heavily on the competent and enthusiastic work of graphic artist Susan Cronin-Paris, who is responsible for the design and production. Harry Wessenberg proof-read the final copy. And Nancy Olsen offered sound advice during each stage of the project. My thanks and appreciation to you all.

Carol O'Hare, Editor and Publisher